Suzi QUATRO
THROUGH MY EYES

Suzi Quatro has always hit the mark, right on target. But when she started in the business and began trying out her ideas, it was a very different time for young girls.

The music business wasn't open to a girl like her, but she was always fighting and trying to be true to herself.

It seems, with this sweet book of reminiscence, that she's being even more true to herself, and for herself. Brava, Suzi!

– Debbie Harry

Suzi QUATRO
THROUGH MY EYES
Poetry & Reminiscences

Second Edition
Published 2016
NEW HAVEN PUBLISHING LTD
www.newhavenpublishingltd.com
newhavenpublishing@gmail.com

The rights of Suzi Quatro, as the author of this work, have been asserted
in accordance with the *Copyrights, Designs and Patents Act 1988.*

All rights reserved. No part of this book may be re-printed or reproduced or utilized
in any form or by any electronic, mechanical or other means, now unknown or
hereafter invented, including photocopying, and recording, or in any information
storage or retrieval system, without the written permission of
the Author and Publisher.

Copyright © 2016 Suzi Quatro
All rights reserved
ISBN:
ISBN: 978-1-910705-39-1

Suzi Quatro has been a household name since 1973, when she screamed her way into the public consciousness with her first No. 1 record, *Can The Can*.

Long before The Spice Girls were even a twinkle in their mothers' eyes, Suzi was the original Girl Power icon. She kicked open the door for all the female lead singers of the past four decades.

Suzi went on to sell 55 million records, star alongside The Fonz in Happy Days, take the title role in the stage version of Annie Get Your Gun and host her own long-running BBC Radio 2 series.

Today, she lives with her husband Rainer near Chelmsford in the UK. Their love-match is celebrated in Through My Eyes' final poem: You Are My Dream Come True.

'I was the first rock'n'roll chick, lead singer, serious bass player, kicking ass with the guys in the band, and beating them at their own game.'

But when the lights go down and the leather catsuit comes off, there's another side of Suzi Quatro that only her closest friends know — a sensitive, soul-searching and philosophical woman who's been pouring her heart out in poetry since she was seven years old. Only no one's had the chance to read it . . . until now.

Through My Eyes is Suzi Quatro's first collection of poetry. It is a collection that is candid, thoughtprovoking, revealing and sometimes shocking. If you thought being an international rock star was all glamour and good times, **Through My Eyes** will take you on a rock'n' rollercoaster of a journey through a life bedevilled by men who were often unsuitable, unspeakable or unattainable ... not that Suzi was going to take any of that lying down!

The poems reveal some of Suzi's deepest and most intimate feelings. They are predominantly about love, from the optimism and exuberance of a young singer about to launch her solo career, to the acrimony and disillusionment relating to various relationships — real, imaginary or longed-for — that punctuated her subsequent life.

Suzi has also included notes that reveal where she was and what she was doing at the time she was writing. Taking things on a stage from her autobiography, **Unzipped**, this is rhyme . . . with a reason!

Contents

Prologue	15
A Good Catholic Girl	17
Love and War	19
Love and War (Lyrics)	21
Between Hell and Midnight	23
'Twas Only the Once We Met	25
Surrender	27
A Bridge to Nowhere	29
Ode to Circumstance	31
Victim of Circumstance (Lyrics)	33
The Scream Inside	35
A Mother	37
A Position of Trust	39
Boulevard of Broken Dreams	41
Buried Letters	43
Oh, Daddy	45
In Your Room	47
Hey, Rock and Roll Star!	49
Chasing the Storm	51
Love Eludes	53
And so, the Curtain Falls	55
As the Curtain Falls (Lyrics)	57
After a While	59
Round and Round Again	61
Sometimes Love is Letting Go (Lyrics)	63
Marriage	65
Dance in the Shadows	67
Mad in Suburbia	69
Two Souls Collide	71
Is Love Enough?	73
Miami Sunrise	75
In Pursuit of Happiness	77
For Better or Verse	79
It's a Small Wonder	81
Devil of Desire	83
Message from the Gods	85
The Road	87
Heir a Parent	89
Fallen from Grace	91
Waiting	93
Who's to Blame?	95
The Answers We All Seek	97

The Shipwreck 99	Interview 123
The Power is One 101	Shall We Dance? 125
Bitch Goddess 103	Seasons 127
Songs We'll Never Know 105	Solitude 129
Common Denominator 107	Solitude (Lyrics) 131
Commitments 109	Suitcase Lizzie 133
Commitments (Lyrics) 111	Don't be Afraid 135
Gay Paris 113	Many Years Down the Road 137
Do I? 115	Through My Eyes 139
Divine Retribution 117	The Warwick 141
Divine Retribution (Lyrics) 119	Self-Discovery 143
Instigate … Terminate 121	You are My Dream Come True 145

This book is dedicated to all lovers, past and present; children; parents; siblings; girlfriends; boyfriends; husbands and wives; and to the greatest and most difficult love of all: ourselves.

Love is ... a many splintered thing.

This is 1101 Torrey Road — the house where my life began ... the house I never left ... my heart and soul.

Prologue

I've been writing poetry since I was seven — no diary for me! — and I've always been passionate about the written word and everything it encompasses: the rhythm, the rhyme, the revelation, the dark, the light, the mystery and the emotion …

I love everything about this very private and fascinating form of communication. I have always found it to be a great comfort to put pen to paper and see where it takes me.

Journalists, friends, songwriting partners and TV interviewers have been kind enough to tell me over the years that I have a poetic turn of phrase — so, taking their compliments on board, I'm finally releasing my words from their secret hiding place … and hoping all those people were right!

There are a few poems here that I wrote at a very young age. They are no less poignant for that. As I take you down the road of my life, you'll read poems about good days, bad days, and the days that were so bad that the only release I could find was to put them down on paper and try to turn a negative into a positive. You may find some poems (and one in particular) disturbing, though not as disturbing as it was for me … I lived it! Mostly, the poems are concerned with the many faces and facets of love. There is heartache, pain, trauma, regret, relief, humour, excitement and sheer joy. This is something we all share, in the spotlight or out of it.

While I hope you'll reserve your right as a reader to interpret the poems as you think fit, I've included some notes for each one, giving an insight into what was going on in my life at the time I wrote it, sometimes explaining, and sometimes not. A woman must have some secrets.

Although I set out to create a book of poetry and no more, I couldn't resist adding the odd personal picture to go with the notes. And so the book took on a life of its own.

Unintentionally, the result seems to have become a minor extension of my autobiography, Unzipped. It is every bit as honest.

The collection covers 55 years of my life. It includes four song lyrics that began life as poems, plus one poem — the last — that I wrote while this book was in the process of being edited, very shortly before publication.

I believe in straight talking — telling it like it is. Anyone who bought this expecting flowery rhymes like moon, June and swoon is reading the wrong book!

I was quite young when I wrote this poem, in 1969, two years before I ended up in London. I was raised on guilt, and I still say my Catholic prayers at night, remembering to bless everyone.

I'm always making deals with the Man Upstairs: I'll do this if you let me do that.

All in all though, it's good to know where the boundaries are. Promise I'll be good from now on — or maybe not!

• *This 1975 picture is from the Welcome To My Nightmare tour of the USA as Alice Cooper's guest. Nice legs! Don't know why I never wore skirts.*

A Good Catholic Girl

A good Catholic girl
In a whirlpool of desire
Trapped!

A mass of contradictions:
When she's good, she's good
When she's bad, she's great!

Her own sense of time
Her own right and wrong
Her own rhythm
A system that's allowed

What's not allowed, she pursues
Despite consequences

Then, in a darkened cubicle
All is revealed
All is forgiven

The rhythm of lust
Beats slow and steady
And touches
A good Catholic girl

A marriage winding down, floundering, confused. This is one of my favourites. All the words came out exactly right and I didn't really have to work on it. I put a pencil in my hand, poised over a blank piece of paper, and it wrote itself.

It became a wonderful song which we performed live for a few years, the first time being on our 1989 tour of Russia where we played to more than half a million people. They used to cheer after the opening line.

There is a demo recording of it — and who knows, it may end up on the anthology.

Love and War

Is it for sadness I yearn
So sweetly?
Once Spring graced my morning
Briefly
Now I linger on a memory

Was the peace I knew
Just a silent war
Behind enemy lines?
Was I a prisoner
Of cowardice
Making do?
No warmth would suffice

If love is war and war is love
If wounded warriors die
Who's after love, who comes before
If war is love and love means war?

And here are the lyrics for the song — again, interesting to note what made it from the poem. Scanning for a melody line is a totally different rhythm.

I love both the poem and the song. It was one of the few songs I wrote on guitar and the riff I came up with for this is very difficult to play. Very few guitarists can do it, and I've had complaints!

I put it down to not being very good on the instrument and making do with my knowledge. It's totally wrong technique-wise, but totally right feeling-wise ... which should be applied to everything in life.

• *This picture was taken in Wales around 1974. Looking out over the ocean of my life, and what do I see?*

Love and War

[QUATRO / WOLFE]

Love and war
Who is the enemy?
I lay my body on the bed of Bastille
Ah ah ah
Forgotten refugee
Love is the enemy you use as your shield
Ah ah ah

Was the memory a peace I knew
Or just a silent war?
Behind enemy lines
I was your prisoner
In the cage of your heart
I should have known from the start
It was love and war
Heard it all before

[SPOKEN]
The lines have been drawn (love and war and love and war)
Beggars and thieves
Will fight to the dawn
You beg for the reasons to believe
Then you steal from them all

You claim you love me (ha ha ha)
But it's hate that I saw
How many ways did we die in this act of war?
Love and war

You got to find a way
Does it matter what we say?
Words to stake the claim
Who dares wins
Love and war

Love and war
Who is the enemy?
I lay my body on the bed of Bastille
Ah ah ah
Forgotten refugee
Love is the enemy you use as your shield

Who's after love? Who comes before?
If war is love … and love is war?
Ah ah ah

When you stop talking, that's it. There are two ways to communicate: talking to each other, or talking at each other. When I wrote this, we were definitely doing the latter.

I'm a pretty strong girl, but the one thing that can kill me is to not be heard. Whether I was or wasn't doesn't really matter; the point is that I felt like I wasn't, and I was dying.

But there's always that nagging doubt. Was I wrong? Should I try harder? Two horses pulling the cart together, and all that.

I guess being crazy would give me a legitimate way out of the situation I was in, as I wouldn't be responsible for myself. But in the end I always have to live by my 11th Commandment: Thou shalt not bullshit thyself.

Between Hell and Midnight

You never talk to me any more … never
Talk at me, sure
Spewing forth great views from above
So certain of my response
Never considering, even for a moment
I might have an opinion

Independent? Oh, yes!
And clever, too
I can analyse an armchair
Right into the ground

But can't quite work this out
This nonentity
Not here, not there
Between Hell and Midnight

And it's driving me crazy … crazy … crazy
Now, there's a point:
Am I?

This was written during a wilderness in my heart ... somewhere between being in love and settled, yet wanting the unobtainable.

I am an in-control person, so when the universe dictates that I will be out of control, I love it!

This encounter hit me over the head like a sledgehammer. I fell into love/lust — who knows what it's called? — but whatever it is or was, it was out of my control. Yet, sadly, it never came to fruition.

I sometimes look back on it and wonder what the Hell it was, where the Hell it came from, was it even real ... and what was the point?

Was I supposed to learn something? Chemistry is just too simple an answer. Was it right? Probably not. Would it have lasted? Probably not. Still, I can dream ... can't I?

• *A 1958 pic of me and neighbour Johnny Reven. I rarely played with girls.*

'Twas Only the Once We Met

'Twas only the once we met
Kindred souls
Never forget
Twined in passage, through tests of time
Secret message within the rhyme
Tell me, my heart, is this our crime?
'Twas only the once we met

Cold light of day intrudes
Moments of bliss
Sweet interludes
As reality looms
I hold on tight
To this fantasy's flight
Cold light of day intrudes

'Twas only the once we met
'Tis the once I cannot forget

One of those poems where the verse is nothing like the way I speak. It just flowed out this way. I sometimes read it and wonder where the Hell it came from.

I was starving, that's for sure. Definitely felt like I was being thrown a crumb to exist on when I needed the entire loaf. But I'm not the kind to surrender. It's not in my vocabulary.

Surrender

Shall I cower on sanity's edge
Or honour vanity's pledge?
Is woman life's great pretender
Her dignity, pain to remember?
Surrender, surrender,
    Surrender

Shoot the beast, still my defender
Share my feast, harvest me, then render
Me hopeless, one small sacrifice
With barely a kiss to suffice
Surrender, surrender,
    Surrender

Shall I trample my dreams thereunder
Or steal his fire and thunder?
And when sated fill another cup
And scream it, yes, scream it:
    Don't give up!
    Surrender!
    Don't ever
    Surrender!

Written in 1989 after a trip back to Detroit to try to sort my feelings out. We've all been there: afraid to leave, afraid to stay.

In my heart, divorce was an ugly word, and one I never thought would be in my vocabulary. I took a long time to make up my mind, which women do ... then, once they have made up their minds, there's no turning back.

I've always been a walking thinker ... or is it a thinking walker? Whatever, this walk definitely did me some good. Decision made. Life moves on. But ponder this: are we any closer to our destination?

I think I'll just keep walking.

• *Linda Theuerkorn, my next-door neighbour and best friend since I was four, is pictured here in Detroit in 1979 at a party in my honour.*

A Bridge to Nowhere

Building bridges to nowhere
Naive
Simple
Pure
It's not so easy to do
The cynics raise their heads
And claim another victim

Love begins it
Life ends it
Till it's hard to remember
Where the journey began

Building bridges to nowhere
And you walk
And walk
And walk

This is one of my favourite poems, and became one of my favorite songs. But I'm going to plead the Fifth Amendment here ...

Ode to Circumstance

Sometimes a moment passes and I think I'm doing okay
Then, from out of nowhere
You flash through my mind,
And lodge yourself in my heart

When I think of you
Allowing my senses to enjoy
I realise how much is missing from my life

There so much I want to say
So much I never do
It comes rushing out in abrupt statements
Like a dog, barking at an intruder
Circumstance is our intruder

I want to see you always
You never leave my thoughts
I make do with memories and phone calls
Both sorry substitutes

I miss the electric force
Going from eye to eye
It's got a life all its own
And nothing we say or do
Can make a difference

Those pauses in conversation
Making love, without touching
God ... so good
Like floating on a sea of orgasmic delight
Sometimes I can't stand it
This good kind of hurt
As all special things are

Be my lover ... you are my love
Please always be my friend
I'm always here for you
Someday, if there's any justice in the world
We will be together

I'll still have that look in my eyes
And a lonely heart on my sleeve
Wait for me

This was recorded for the CMC album "Latest And Greatest", and we did it live for quite a while.

No more information available! Go to your imagination, please ... and stay tuned.

• *I look ready for battle in this picture from the Russian tour. It was 1989 and Glasnost was just beginning — not just for the country, for me too.*

Victim of Circumstance

[Quatro]

Lovers pass by, then suddenly you're on my mind
Got the power, you still got control of me
Far away seems long ago
I compromised
Better the Devil you know
Now there's silence in my soul

Chorus
Victim of circumstance
Life is a game of chance
And we just go on believing
What we need to survive
But if there's nothing more, what's everyone searching for?
When love's angel comes a-knocking at your door
Will you be alone?

Heartaches come and go
Each time I think of you I know
We had something rare
It's still got a hold of me
You came into my world
Changed my perception with a single word
Life is everything, love complete

Bridge
We follow, trapped in our destiny
Never knowing what tomorrow may bring

Chorus

Took a trip back home in 1989 and stayed with my parents at their house.

It was two years before my divorce. I asked my parents to please leave me alone, and they did.

I drove every day, everywhere — schools, shopping malls, old friends' houses — trying to tap back into the girl who left home all those years ago.

I hope I came back a stronger person

The Scream Inside

Running away
A break
Some space
Necessary for my sanity

I walked aimlessly
Around familiar haunts
Searching for clues
Searching for the little girl full of dreams

No-one had any answers
No-one knew anything but me
Still I shared some of my pain

Now I'm returning
To face the issues
Without the anger … I hope
Still, I suppose
A little anger is good

Roll on, London!

This was written around 1988 and oh, what a story! I've always needed my mother desperately. She said that when I was young I was so shy. Me! Can you believe it?

I wrote this as a tribute, in a funny/sad kind of way. She didn't have much happiness in her life — only through her children, whom she would have died for. I wanted to address this in verse. I had this printed and put into a frame with a picture of her holding me as a two-year-old. Next time I visited her in Dallas, where she finished her days, the frame I gave her held a very nice publicity picture of me instead.

"What happened, Mom?" I asked. "Where did my poem go?" And her reply? "It was such a waste of a pretty frame."

Mom, that says it all. I love you every day.

• Mom's pictured holding me, aged 6 months. In my heart, I never left Detroit. Her favourite song, by the way, was the Chaplin classic, "Smile".

A Mother

A mother's face
One more cradle to rock
A mother's place
Cold heart to unlock
Day after day
No pleasure in sight
Is there no way
To ease her plight?
A silent space
No door to knock

A lonely smile
Sweeps her broom
Dust of emptiness
Fills the room
Pictures of children
Share the wall
Night after night
Shadows fall
On barren seeds
Within her womb

A mother's face
So soft to touch
Was it my disgrace
I needed so much?

Ooooh, was I angry! I wrote a lot in the decision years, the period between 1986 and 1991. I was arguing with myself, arguing with my man, arguing with everyone — not happy, and definitely very angry!

The funny thing is, I'm the epitome of *Girl Power* and have been since *Day One*. But within that power lies a pleaser — part conditioning, part being a female, part being an entertainer, and part being a *Gemini* who's able to play whatever role the recipient requires ... usually to her own detriment.

It takes almost a lifetime to stand up and be exactly who you are: no games, no bullshit, standing naked, good and bad parts exposed. Finally, I fought back.

A Position of Trust

A long time ago
I put you in a position of trust
My heart was in your hands
You abused it
And you abused me

Forever parading your virility
Trampling all over my self-respect
How the Hell was I supposed to protect myself —
With my looks, with my body,
Or the brains I left under the pillow?

Got news for ya, Honey:
You may have wanted a sex symbol
But you got me
And I want blood!

I had a model for this poem – somebody very, very close to me – but she shall remain anonymous. She knows who she is, anyway. And although she may have been the model, I've met many others, male and female, who fit this description.

I've always felt sorry for anyone who bases their entire existence on their looks. The danger is what happens when the looks go. Who are you then?

How scary it must be when you go to the well and the well is empty.

She gave up everything for her moment in the sun but, like Icarus, her wings melted.

• *Mom with daughters Patti, me and Arlene, in Patti's LA home in 1990-91, Mom's last good year.*

Boulevard of Broken Dreams

Down the Boulevard of Broken Dreams
Dancing to tunes she'll never sing
Down the Boulevard of Broken Dreams
Shining stars leave her crying in the wings

She pouts her lips, draws black lines
Powdering cracks of passing time
Hips swaying to and fro
Skin-tight skin shaking
To the shapes she's in

Eyelashes long, smile too bright
The boys get younger
Ships in the night
Parading her youth, eternal tease
Making her age, with flamboyant ease

Painful to remember
Hard to forget
Yesterday's road
Of no regrets

And she keeps on walking
She just keeps on walking

Down the Boulevard of Broken Dreams
Dancing to tunes she'll never sing
Down the Boulevard of Broken Dreams
Shining stars leave her crying in the wings

Forbidden fruit, a long time ago. The relationship was not allowed. But there's no better way to convince myself that something's exactly what I want than for somebody to say no ... in this case, the recipient of this verse.

I couldn't persuade, I couldn't convince, but it didn't stop me from trying. And, of course, the million-dollar question: if this person had said yes, would we be together today?

I doubt it. The reasons were valid; I just didn't want to see them. But beware: my bite's still worse than my bark! I'm leaving my options open here.

Buried Letters

I won't break, I won't die
I'm too strong for that

But without you
I will truly forfeit
My chance of happiness

I am determined to be together
Some how, some day, some way

I'm coming to get you
With nothing but love in my heart
Beware, my bite is worse than my bark

I want you to a dangerous degree
Say yes
And I'll sleep on the dream every night

To my father. Obviously, I had issues — valid ones. Now both my parents are gone and it all seems such a waste of time and emotion. Life is so short after all. But then again, maybe not. I think it's important, as we're finding out who we are, to be honest about our feelings.

I was a troubled soul a lot of the time when I was young. We were so many ... five children, all wanting that extra piece of attention. And I always seemed to need that little bit more than the others.

This is an honest account of how I felt about my father for a very long time ... right up until he was almost gone. I started to see things differently, and made my peace — and then he was gone.

I love you, Dad. You were a very special man. And thank you for everything you gave me.

Oh, Daddy ...

2am ... a bottle of Port
And, a paragraph in someone's life
I stop ... and think
Eyes wet ... just a little
God, I wish you were here

I'd say it all
What I think of life
Mine ...
Theirs ...
Yours ...
Ours ...

The relationship we have
The relationship we haven't
Lost moments never shared
Yes, alcohol breaks down walls, then ...
Spews all, no feelings spared

I love you
I wish you understood who I am

Oh what talks we'd have
Reshape destiny, even!
Discuss success
How I handled it
How you wish I'd handled it
Haggle over money, houses never bought
Family not supported
Arguing morals, ideals

Husbands, children ...
Things I fought for
Things I thought I did right
We'd argue on into night
And when morning broke
Strangers once more

A bottle of Port
And a paragraph in someone's life
Eyes get wet, just a little ...
Oh, Daddy ...

Written just after I last gave birth, in 1985. I was deep into motherhood but very alone — so alone that I made my nanny my best friend.

My career was on hold, and I was scared that my time was over. File this under "feeling sorry for myself".

In Your Room

When tales have been told
The goods sold
Who then claims the prize?
Images wane
Memories, pain
Reflect deep in green eyes

You stay inside your room
You lay thinking
Alone in your doom
In the darkness of dreams
Once again you can be
The hero
So let the games resume

Walls hung with gold
From young into old
Leather protecting your heart
Smiles that disguise
The heartache of time
Feeling a bit left out

And you stay inside your room
You lay thinking
Alone in your gloom
In the darkness of dreams
Once again you can be
The hero
So let the games resume

I was 12 years old when I wrote this ... and, as you can see in the picture, I had attitude, even then!

It was a very strange thing to write at that age, but I think I always knew that success had a price.

I always had my eye on the big apple ... it was the only path I was interested in. I had to create, had to communicate, had to be me.

Mom saved this poem, finally bringing the long-forgotten verse to me on her last trip to the UK. She died the following year.

Hey, Rock and Roll Star!

It didn't take much
To make you believe again
Now that the depression is over

You're all wound up
And the people are cheering
And the people want you
And the people love you
It didn't take much

I feel so very young

A pretty recent one ... probably about five years ago. I was trying to put this to a song, but it didn't fit. It's better as a poem.

This is all about feeling comfortable in your own skin. It can take a lifetime. Some people don't find it until they are out of their skin and in the ground. Luckily, I found me. As it says, my jeans are torn, the edges are frayed. I've been chasing my storm.

Chasing the Storm

Electric flash in the silver rain
Desert sands kind of soothe my pain
Jump back, in my skin
I've come back to within
And I'm feeling good

Southern Comfort trying to comfort me
Cowboy boots, threadbare seams
Talking to my mind
Walking to unwind
And I'm feeling good

My jeans are torn, the edges are frayed
I've been chasing the storm
Chasing the storm

Mercedes ride in a rear-view mirror
Long white line, the road from here
Heartbreak, don't destroy me
True love, come and find me
And I'm feeling good

Washed-out blues in a turquoise trance
Desperado does a naked dance
Jump back in my skin
I've come back to within
And I'm feeling good

I have a very good friend whose mother died when he was very young. I feel it shaped his destiny and sexuality totally, though he would deny this.

A mother is the most important person in a child's life, for every reason including nurturing, teaching, holding, feeding, inspiring, giving security, and offering unconditional love. God, the list is endless!

When you rip this away from someone so young, it must be devastating. I had mine until I was 41, and it still nearly killed me.

• *My brother Michael is pictured here at Hyde Hall in 2001. He played the piano for my guests, and reduced one and all to tears. He is that good.*

Love Eludes

A soft touch, a sweet smell
Brushing his hair tenderly
And he loved her ... oh so much

God's perfect union
Mother ... son ...
Then desertion

She's gone, she's gone
She's gone
What's done is done

He locked himself away
For hours on end
The boy must die
No-one will hurt him again

God's perfect union
Mother ... son ...
Then desertion

Love eludes

One of my favourites, this was written during our last Australian tour together in 1990.

It was a very difficult tour for both of us for different reasons. I was so very unhappy and spent my time writing my feelings down, which ended up either in a song or a poem. This one became both poem and song.

Words just flowed out of me like a bleeding wound that wouldn't stop. Looking way back at it now from the grand old age of 62, it has a kind of poetic justice.

He never changed, God bless him. He was who he was, is what he is, and always will be. In a crazy kind of way, you have to respect that.

He was permanently on 11 — and I guess I should have worn earplugs.

And so, the Curtain Falls

And so the curtain falls
Applause dies away
Crowds leave the stalls
One bulb lights the stage

One minute more, I stand
Listening to the sound
Of silence, once a roar
I feel myself come down

As warmth begins to fade
I turn into the dark
I know what price I've paid
Success has left its mark

And so the curtain falls
On one more lonely star
You never heard me call
So loud was your guitar

And now the song. It always interests me to see how a poetic verse changes to scan with a melody.

I was never quite happy with the tune I wrote around it. It was finally recorded in 2004-05, but not released. I worked with the guitarist Al Hodge on the unreleased album just before "Back to the Drive". Some of the tracks were re-recorded, but this one was not.

Al loved these lyrics. He took them home and wrote the tune, and it's a goodie. But Al isn't with us any more. I guess I'd better get this song on to CD or he'll be haunting me.

God bless you, Al. If anyone could understood these words, you could. I hope you're in the band up there and singing with angels.

• My close friend and long-time collaborator Mike Chapman, his wife Zan, me and my husband Rainer in 2010, celebrating my 60th birthday at Motown studios in Detroit.

As the Curtain Falls

[Quatro / Hodge]

And so the curtain falls, applause dies away
As crowds leave the stalls, one bulb lights the stage
I stand one minute more, in silence once a roar
And I feel myself coming down
The warmth begins to fade, I turn into the dark
You know what price we've paid, the road has left its mark
And I stand here all alone, God, how time has flown
And I see myself coming down

Chorus
And as the curtain falls on everything we are
It's just one more lonely night, in one more low-lit bar
And one more lonely lady, wishing on a star
Guess you never heard me call, so loud was your guitar

Long-distance calls in the middle of the night
Another empty hall, no relief in sight
As I reach out to touch, this distance is too much
I can't stop myself looking round
Cheap hotel rooms, smoking cigarettes
Saying I love you, things I can't forget
And I lay here feeling low, another town, another show
I can't help myself feeling down

Chorus

As the curtain falls on one more lonely star
As the curtain falls, you keep playing your guitar
As the curtain falls, on everything we are
I'm just one more lonely lady, wishing on a star
As the curtain falls, you keep playing your guitar

If you've read my autobiography, "Unzipped", you'll know who this is ... my first real grown-up love, something you never forget.

I also wrote the song "Wiser Than You" for this man. He was how I judged love for a long, long time.

I was so afraid that nothing would ever measure up again, and I'd be alone and lonely (don't know which is worse) for the rest of my life. And I was only 21!

It was 1971 and I was in New York, waiting for my flight to London to begin my solo career. I'd just seen him again, and was wondering if it would be the last time.

It was ... for many years. Then, in the late Nineties, and with the blessing of my husband, we had a drink in the bar of the Miami hotel we were staying at.

No Miami sunrise was forthcoming that time; just a hello and a goodbye, like the poem says.

After a While

After a while
I'll probably see you again
Maybe I'll pretend to know you
Or treat you like an old friend
We'll talk of silly nothings
And be so very kind
Afraid to look at each other
For the love we might find
After a while, after a while

When I do see you again
Walking down some street
I'll be alone, and so will you
We'll stop in the middle
While the world turns on for us

Then turns off
Cuz somewhere along the way
We lost the courage to love
After a while

I'll probably see you again
After a while … after a while

At some point, every artist must feel like a money machine. It was even worse for me because, as a woman, I had the children and raised the children, and it was my name that brought the money in. So basically the workload, responsibility, everything, was all down to me.

It wasn't easy. I never truly resented it until the children were about four and six when it all started to look very one-sided.

I started to think, "What about me?" So this tirade would have been written in about 1988 ... three years before my one-way ticket to freedom.

• *Close friend Chris Most and me are pictured at dinner at her house in 1990, the year of Mom's last trip to the UK.*

Round and Round Again

The big guy takes a fall
He nearly fooled 'em all
A fool on Dollar Hill
I run on his treadmill
And we go round and round again

I built him far too tall
Inside my mental wall
Soft words, never spoke
Suddenly I awoke
And we go round and round again

The big guy cannot see
A forest for the tree
This fool who cannot find
A way inside my mind
And we go round and round again

One of the best lyrics and songs Shirlie Roden and I came up with. We really hit the nail on the head.

    I do this on stage sometimes, and it was in my one-woman show "Unzipped" as the last song before I left the stage to change clothes.

    It was written like a three-act play. We were really on form in my creating room that day.

Sometimes Love is Letting Go

[Quatro / Roden]

My Mama always told me
If you truly love someone
Don't hold on too tight
Sometimes love is letting go

Sometimes love is letting go
You've fallen hard, even though
He shows you nothing in return
But you still give everything
Cuz you've yet to learn
That if he's yours, one day he'll know
Sometimes love … is letting go

You know, my Dad always told me that men don't show their feelings easy
So I said Hey, Dad, the times I've seen you cry
Have been the most precious to me
Sometimes love is letting go

Sometimes love is letting go
And when you're scared, scared to let love show
And so afraid, your heart will break
Just let it happen, for your heart's sake
Sweet emotion, you got to let it flow
Sometimes love … is letting go

And when I finally grew up, I fell in love, but it didn't last
We just didn't belong together any more, and I had to be strong
And say to myself Hey, Girl, sometimes love is letting go

Sometimes love … is letting go
We were flying high, now I'm lying low
In your arms like a stranger, you feel so cold
The truth is plain, but rarely told
You gotta stop saying yes, when you mean no
And if he's yours one day he'll know
Sweet emotion, you gotta let it flow
Sometimes love … is letting go

This was early on, probably around 1986-87. My discontent was creeping in slowly under the facade and starting to show, just around the edges.

I wasn't ready to face full-on failure, but addressed my doubts anyway. I was still hoping to fall back in love and make it work ... anything to avoid the dreaded D-word.

Interesting how I ended it by suggesting that if she were free of barriers, a single rose could grow. I am free, I did grow, and I'm growing still.

• *My son Richard is pictured here in 1991. Too cute for his own good.*

Marriage

A fifty-fifty contract
Life's blood, in red we write
In sickness for all we lack
May another provide, despite

Bargain, lock those chains
Prisoner to our needs
Choke, stale air we breathe
Within this cage, we bleed

Possession cannot prosper
Nor flourish side by side
Obsession, it will falter
For he swims against her tide

And if she sees through darkness
One bright and burning light
Will she realise his madness
And set her wings in flight?

A fifty-fifty contract
Is it silence partners fear?
Her strength, all he lacked
Laid bare, without her near

A marriage built on weakness
Cannot rise about its mire
Nor heal the inner illness
Or satisfy heart's desire

Were she free of barriers
A single rose could grow
So this princess and her warrior
Could reap the love they sow

Written at the beginning of an affair. Had not made up my mind yet to take that leap of faith.

    I have a golden rule: I must be told, "I love you," first. In this instance it didn't happen, and the affair bit the dust.

    Rule number one: follow your own rules.

Dance in the Shadows

If we dance in the shadows
Surrender to desire
If by chance you begin to burn
Could I put out your fire?

If my heart should start breaking
From the look in your eyes
Could I give all you're taking?
Would I tell you no lies?

Could we?
Should we?
Dance in the shadows?

In this confused state of mind, in 1986, I fell in love with every passing stranger, imagining the entire chase/catch scenario.

I love the feeling of being in love; it's the air I breathe, and any fantasy will do!

Be careful, the next one might be you ...

• *I love photo booths. They are so revealing, somehow. I had a lost look in my eyes, and the year was somewhere between 1972 and 1991. You figure it out!*

Mad in Suburbia

Nothing's changed, nothing will
Wait for me
You inspire me, as I do you
We cannot ignore that much longer

Have someone when you need it
I don't mind … I am not jealous
Patience …
I will soon be free to show you
How to make love
With the love of your life

And, when I do
When we are finally as one
You will say all those things
I have been longing to hear

You won't be able to let me go
Ever
I will never leave you
Ever

Doing what is right hurts
Trying not to break too many hearts
Breaks mine every single day

I know you are frightened of pushing me
Because decisions made in heated moments
Are not to be trusted

So you sit and say nothing
I sit and say everything
Slowly going mad
In suburbia

Written around the same time as "'Twas Only the Once We Met". No matter how pretty the words are, the reality is that nothing happened.

It could just be that unfinished business is the best architect for poetry ...

Two Souls Collide

When two souls collide, it's beyond all control
Emotion in motion, we must go with the flow
Am I scared to death? What madness is this?
Sweet bliss is mine, with nary a kiss

From poets to lovers, two hearts admit defeat
King, build me a castle, within our deepest dreams
And lay me down softly, so I may sleep

For when I awaken, my lion will roar
And I will be your queen once again, for ever more

When two souls collide, they know what they know
When two souls collide, they must go whither they go

I found a book store in Melbourne, Australia, called The Hill Of Content, that saved my life on that last tour we did as husband and wife in 1990.

I actually bought scented poetry books and read them aloud while travelling to the gigs with the band. You can imagine how well this went down with certain people on the journey.

This poem is a direct result of all that reading, soaking in and coming out of my heart and soul, and my situation at that time.

I still love those books which are beside my bed at home. I open them, smell them and read from them, with a totally different agenda — not survival, just pleasure.

Oh, what a little time can do for the weary soul.

• *This is my favourite picture: Me, Laura, and Richard (in my tummy) in 1984. The word here is contented.*

Is Love Enough?

Is love enough to carry me
To sensual delights?
Or will the need bury me
In restless, senseless fights?

Is love enough to share the load
Or heal the child inside?
Or is this never-ending road
The road where something's died?

Is love enough? I hope to see
Two arms that only give
And if you reach out slowly
Love is enough … to live

Many years later, while reading my poem "After a While", I had the idea for this song based on my memories of that love affair.

I really thought I was the only one carrying a torch all these years. As it turned out, after we reacquainted, we exchanged a few e-mails and he sent me a poem he'd written for us 20 years earlier ... same title, almost the same words, same everything. How amazing is that?

It's nice to know we both had the same precious memory of our time together. Whenever I'm in Miami, which is often, I go to the beach and think "This is where my life changed." Love is ... a many splintered thing.

Miami Sunrise

That still Miami sunrise, casting shadows in the sand
You gazed into my soul, I smiled and held your hand
So terrified, mystified … all so new to me
As the tide washed over us, we pledged eternity

I remember how we kissed, as we melted into one
Music in the waves, two children in the sun
A whirlwind of emotion, caught in time ever more
Soon to be forgotten, two strangers on the shore

That still Miami sunrise, a moment we shared
It seems so long ago, we touched, we cared
Now so far apart, I send love from this distant heart
That still Miami sunrise, a moment we dared

We found an empty bar room in that hotel by the sea
I sat so close there was no space between you and me
I begged you to release me — electric, so strong
Your gold ring burned my finger, we knew this was wrong

Yes, the love of my life — so tender, so sweet
I gave everything I had, surrender complete
And that moment belongs to us
For ever more

We stumbled to the bed, bathed in twilight's finest hour
You blossomed in my arms like a rare, precious flower
We could not know our fate, we cannot guess destiny
Waves roll in and wash away
What was not meant to be

This was actually written upon awakening — and I don't want to explain. Otherwise I might as well have filmed it and put it online — X-rated, of course. A girl has to have some secrets!

Think "Gone with the Wind", when Rhett finally carries Scarlett upstairs and has his way with her ... then, in the morning, there's a close-up, just on her, waking up and remembering the night before. She rolls her eyes and smiles, then, remembering the best part, giggles and blushes. And there you have it: enjoy!

• *Rainer is pictured here in New York. Judging by the haircut, it must have been around 1995.*

In Pursuit of Happiness

Let go … let me go
I must go
Someone awaits me elsewhere
You insist
I resist
You excite
I, despite myself
Turn softly into your love
Licking
Biting
Touching
Never quite kissing

I can't stay but a moment
Oh..!
What's missing
In someone else's arms

In pursuit of happiness
My heart leads
And I must follow
Wherever it may go

(WRITTEN UPON AWAKENING)

This was the hardest poem to write, but I had to get it out of my system. So sad, so true. It denotes our last time together.

In fact, it's still so raw that I actually considered not putting it into the book, but that would be wrong.

This is my poetry, these are my deepest feelings, and they don't go much deeper or much painful that this.

My God, what we women do sometimes when we feel we should! Even the most liberated of us bows to conditioning. And yet, I don't regret it. We could not have ended any other way, and it made me very sure that I was making the right decision. I was finally able to walk, and keep on walking.

I am walking still, through the pages of my life ... wherever the journey may take me.

For Better or Verse

Lay back softly, softly
It won't take long
Tongues trade touches
One touch too strong

Giver meets her taker
Lost upon lust's bed
For now he will take her
And fuck with her head

Many ways to abuse
Sweet words of devotion
No life left to choose
Devoid of emotion

Face pressed in the pillow
Back against the wall
Bend over, a weeping willow
Feel nothing, nothing at all

Take me, my darling
Break me right in two
Destroy guilty conscience
And when I say adieu

No tears will I cry
No sweet despair
No more lay, nor lie
For broken minds cannot care

I gave you my body
You wanted my soul
I let you inside
You wanted control

So take me, my darling
It's time you were spent
All my hopes for tomorrow
One chance, Heaven sent

I gave this poem to friends with children. How wonderful children are. They do change your life.

After writing this, and framing this 1986 picture of my two, I thought what a nice gift it would be, so I had loads printed, framed them, and sent them to my friends.

• *I think it's a beautiful tribute to what love can accomplish at its best.*

It's a Small Wonder

It's a small wonder
Unlike any other
Special gift of God
A loving bundle
Father and mother
Made by each other
Love creates another
Small wonder

(FOR LAURA AND RICHARD)

An old flame, way back when I was young. Ah, but can you define young? He was a Scorpio ... deadly for me! There's a danger there that I'm drawn to like a moth to a flame.

Sometimes when I want to go to sleep I count star signs in my head instead of sheep.

My most frequent boyfriends/lovers throughout my life — by far — have been Scorpios.

Whenever I feel that irresistible pull of lust with no explanation, you bet your sweet ass he's a Scorpio.

Devil of Desire

You stand so alone
In your piercing disguise
Clad in emotionless armour
But the depths of your heart
Alive in your eyes
One look, and I surrendered

You let me reveal
My deepest desires
Cloaked in the arms of a friend
You welcomed my feelings
Fanning the fires of lust
From beginning to end

We met in the middle of fantasy
A mid-life crisis game
We played with the rules of sanity
And nothing was ever the same
He strikes again
This Devil of desire

This was after my Egypt trip – the second poem from this experience. It really opened up another side of me. Crazy or not, I feel I lived there before in another lifetime.

My second husband took me there before we were married and made my dream come true. In fact, he's made a lot of my dreams come true. 1993, first and only trip to Egypt ... wow.. what an experience.

Message from the Gods

Will you go with me down dark tunnels
To the very essence of my being
Where energy funnels
Into spirit
Body and soul
Where we begin as we end
Alone, without a friend?
Will you go with me and light the way?

Written on the road ... which road, which year, who knows? But I've been travelling down it since 1964, counting the white lines, the hotels, the Coke machines, the hamburgers, the sweat, the dives, and the music blasting out of the radio speakers.

So it's simply called "The Road". God bless us all, it's a nasty job ... but somebody has to do it!

The Road

I wish this drive could go on forever
And never reach the other side
So we could throw our fates to the wind
On a never-ending ride

I don't know how we fell into this space
But it's a place that's wild and free
And where it's gonna end, God only knows
But he ain't telling you or me

And the road keeps on rolling
Down the highway of life
And this dream keeps me going
On this highway called Life

If we could freeze our time together
Save it for a rainy day
So we could fill our hearts with pleasure
When nobody wants to play

I wish I had a dime for every single smile
Yes, it's truth that lays us bare
And if we make it last one more mile
It's truth … that will take us there

In the cycle of life, this is a familiar pattern. My parents followed it with me, I followed it with my children, Laura is walking down this familiar road with her child, and Richard's turn will come.

Some things never change. I don't feel hard done by, but blessed. I recently broke my right knee and left wrist, badly, and was on a walker for four months (hit a brick wall actually) and of course it changes you.

My sister Patti came to see me while I was recovering, and we bonded bigtime. Then we met up again about a month later in Detroit while I was doing my documentary for BBC Radio 2. We talked again, picking up where we'd left off — and all of a sudden I was in tears! I could hardly get the words out, I was so choked up. Finally I managed to splutter out: "I didn't make it in spite of my family, I made it because of them."

You may interpret that as you wish. It was a relief to speak those words that I didn't even know I had in me. This is the end result of the poem, and a happing ending. Or maybe it's a happy beginning.

• *Pictured here with my parents in Detroit in 1979 ...soooo cold.*

Heir a Parent

If it's me who makes the world go round
And me who'll carry memories on
If it's me that happiness depends upon
Why do we love at all?

If it's me you sacrificed for
Grew old, worn and haggard for
Stayed up late and waited for
Why do we love at all?

If it's me who made you worry sick
Baby too long, teen too quick
If it's me who made you choose and pick
Why did you meet at all?

But, if it's me who's older now
Makes you smile, sometimes frown
And if it's me who loves you anyhow
That's why we love at all

In that black place ... It was 1990 and I was almost ready to leave my marriage. Again, the Catholic upbringing: angels, Devils ... oh boy!

And to quote one of my favourite songwriters: breaking up is hard to do.

Fallen from Grace

It's Cupid's great plan
In love's scheme of things
There's a no-man's-land
Where angels never sing

Where Satan rules victorious
Black eyes of evil shine
And two hearts duel, precarious
On the edge of cruel and kind

Fallen from grace
A forsaken place
Its boundaries unknown

Fallen from grace
Life's empty space
Face-to-face
We are all alone

Waiting to come to England, Summer of '71. Was due to fly out on 31 October. Counting the days, hours, minutes.

Spent my time writing songs and poems, playing music, daydreaming, riding my bike, sooooo happy.

I was on my way at last. One of my happiest poems, from one of my happiest times. Everything was in front of me, waiting to happen.

• *Pictured here with my granddaughter Amy in 2005 on a boat in the harbour at Hamburg after her first flight.*

Waiting

The sun is so hot
So damn beautifully hot
Wind blows my hair
Into a tangled mess
Then stops, changing its mind
As I drink in the heat
A laughing cloud makes me shiver

Sitting cross-legged
Warm, dreaming
Anything bad is hard to imagine

Sun and winds make me dream
I am content with my life
Still I wait
For the sun and I to become one
So I am able to warm a room
And gently blow my lover's thoughts
Into peaceful slumber
Waiting
Waiting

As the poem says: then I grew up. The key line here is, "Then all of a sudden the woman emerged, without any warning."

How many times does this happen? Must be a lot. We do grow up because we have to. We become mothers. It changes everything.

Either you both grow together as parents and partners, or you grow apart — and who can say who's to blame?

Who's to Blame?

Ripping each other apart
And who can say who's to blame?
We can't go back
And pretend innocence … it's gone
No-one can say where or why
But it's gone
Both of us, a story to tell
A price has been paid
Winner? Loser?
And who can say who's to blame?

I gave my all, tried so hard
Always a compromise
Then, all of a sudden
The woman emerged
Without any warning

You loved so much
Believed, supported
But forgot to hang around
When I needed you most
And now you hurt so bad

Ripping each other apart
And no-one can say who's to blame

Oh boy, do I remember this! It was written on my return flight from Dallas, where I'd flown to see my mother who was undergoing an operation to remove a football-sized cancer in her stomach.

Although the cancer would certainly kill her, the operation would make the rest of her time on Earth a little more comfortable.

I saw one of my nieces at the hospital, the one who'd always had a huge problem with me. It seemed the perfect time to address the issue as I was feeling emotional and vulnerable and wanted to reach out to everyone. So I pulled her into an empty room and said: "Let's do it. Let's have it out, heart to heart. Lay it on the table, say whatever you like and let's look at it and talk about it."

I really wanted to get it fixed if I could. But she had nothing to say. Wow! I then had to go inside myself and find the answers. That's what this poem's about.

• *Dad, Patti, me, Arlene, Mom and Nancy are pictured in Detroit at the time of Dad's bypass in 1984. Richard's in my tummy, growing.*

The Answers We All Seek

What did I learn today?
How did I perceive
Through cloudy eyes of anger
Who was there to see?

So many wrongs upon my soul
Does no-one understand?
God forbid, if I let go
Who will hold my hand?

Will tears I shed release me
From barriers inside?
Of fears, instead, induce me
Keep this ache inside

Pain's been my comfort
Old friend to turn to in need
Heartache … quite a banquet
Foul feast on which I feed

Starve this discontent
Pull out these weeds of hate
Plant one tree of happiness
Sow a different fate

I wish for fields of flowers
Growing 'neath the sun
When God's flowers have blossomed
I'll know I have won

My heart will follow slowly
Footsteps slow and weak
To reach that truth within me
The answers we all seek

This is what I learned today
This is what I've seen
From darkness comes morning
And from love, what life can mean

Again, so hurt. Why do we do it to ourselves? This person (no name) was very important to me for many, many years. But he had a cruel streak.

Usually I gave as good as I got, but in this instance I was beaten emotionally ... at least momentarily. So, I say "You've won" ... but what a shallow victory.

I don't think goodbye was his intention. And before we could fix it, he was gone.

The Shipwreck

Forever falling … into the uncertainties of our existence
What is there to see?
What is there to learn?
With my eyes wide open, I give myself up to this pain
This pain that could never live up to my expectations
Holding on to an outdated loyalty, I wave my little flag
And … surrender

You've won, you bastard, but if I were you
I'd hold tight to that cold, cruel heart, it's all you have
And, if you continue to lose passengers by the boat-load
You will one day become your deepest fear: alone.

God bless you and all who do not wish to sail with you

Goodbye, from a paying passenger

I will take my chances on the lifeboat, before you sink

The trip to Egypt in 1993 was a dream come true. My second husband took me there. We were sightseeing, and suddenly I saw this pyramid.

Acting totally on instinct, I gave the camera to our guide and said: "Take a picture but don't take it until I tell you."

I walked towards the pyramid, and when I felt whatever I was supposed to be feeling, I turned my head back to the camera, facing the pyramid, and said: "Now. Take the picture."

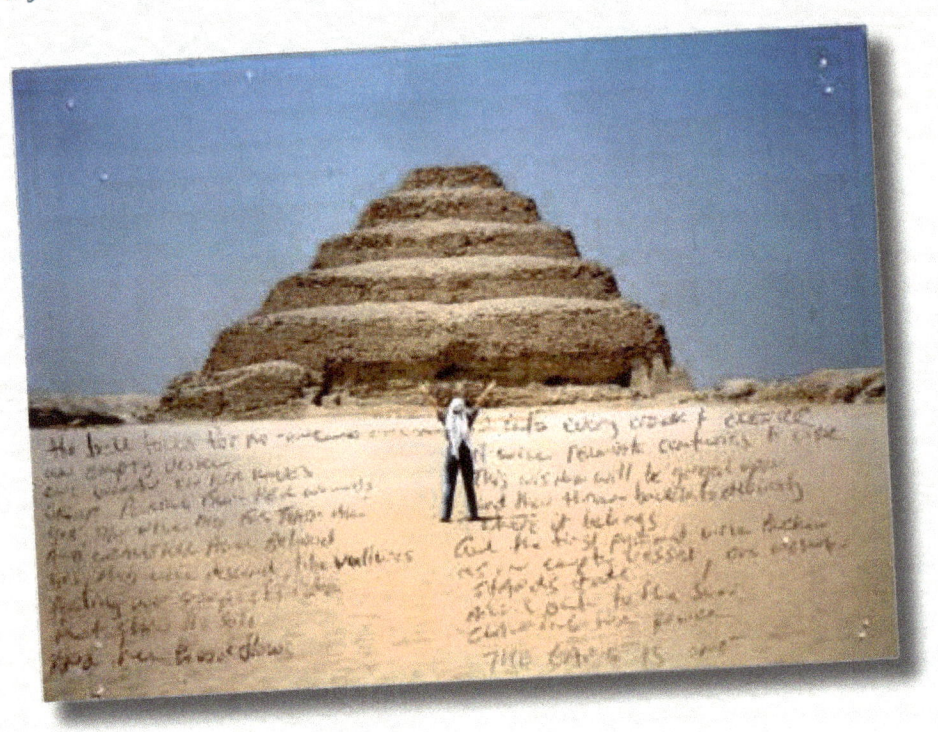

I had my arms stretched right out, and felt this power flowing through me. It was beautiful. There is a picture of that moment.

I wrote this poem down without even thinking about it. I have the poem and the picture blown up and framed in my home..

It was a trip I shall never forget. My entire journey has been all about finding out who I am. — hence the final line, The power is one (ie, you are the power).

The Power is One

The bell tolls for no-one
An empty vessel
One woman, on her knees
Grief pouring from her wounds
Yes, she will die for them all
And leave her power behind
Yes, they will descend … vultures
Feeding over scraps of wisdom
That stain the soil
As her blood flows
Into every crack and crevice
It will permeate centuries to come
This wisdom will be gorged upon
And then thrown back into divinity
Where it belongs
And the first pyramid will beckon
As an empty vessel
One woman stands tall
Arms stretched out to the sun
Claiming her power

The power is one

I'm not a lots-of-girlfriends type of person — one-on-one suits me — so when a friendship goes bust, it's very damaging.

I'm so sensitive — in fact, too sensitive — and when you hurt me, it goes deep. I suppose that goes with the territory of being an artist.

This person shall remain nameless, but she was (and still is) a good friend and had been for almost my entire life. With all true friendships, you can disagree — and we did, bigtime! In fact, it was so big that it had the potential of destroying all we shared.

Here's what happened. I was asked to help, emotionally. I tried, and then it was turned around and used against me. I wasn't happy about it, and I retaliated because I felt I was being attacked. It's not pretty when that happens, and everything gets so negative.

This poem came flying out of my head and heart. Looking at it now the dust has settled, all I can say is that I was very hurt.

The words wouldn't come out any other way ... and to leave the words inside would have killed me.

Bitch Goddess

You mend your curtains with weak stitches
And when drawn, they never quite keep out the cold
How embarrassing, to break open like an egg
Desperately trying to clean up the mess
Before anyone sees

What have I done … what have I done?
Would knowing have made it any easier?
To give all is awesome; to get nothing in return, tragic

I feel for you … I truly do
My shoulder black with your mascara
Ruining my sweater, deep rivers of regret
How sad … how truly sad

Maybe you set your sights too high
Who are you, after all?
Flesh, blood, bones … just like the rest of us
Whose only talent was having the brains
To ride on someone else's coat-tails
And now, like a burned-out comet,
You've come crashing down to Earth
God, is this reality!

Pretending to be the grand lady
Well, it just doesn't work
Try looking in the mirror … see yourself
True compassion is understanding
You have a long way to go

A little word of advice:
Next time you expose yourself
Have a warm emotional blanket ready
To wrap yourself in when it's all over

I am your friend. You're going to miss me

I had a friend — a talented friend — a long time ago. She could have been a star, but it was not to be. This was written as we were getting to know each other as people.

It's sometimes difficult to make friends after you're famous; it distorts reality so. I needed a friend very badly at this time when everything else was crashing in pieces around me, so I let her in.

• This 1989 picture is from my parents' Golden Wedding anniversary. I wrote a song that we performed at the dinner. Well, my sisters performed it because I was crying so hard I couldn't get a note out! This is Arlene, Patti, me and Nancy rehearsing at Nancy's house.

Songs We'll Never Know

Coffee and arrogance
Smiling and innocent
Not impressed at all
A star or two
Won old, one knew
Let's rise before we fall

Songs of pain
Songs of blame
Songs we'll never share
Words debate
Words we hate
Words … we'd never dare

Photographs of faded laughs
Too close for comfort's ease
Autographs on jaded backs
A bridge too far to sea

Coffee and innocence
Losing our arrogance
Too precious to delay
A star or two
Won old, one knew
I think that you're okay

Another lover? Who is it? Aaaah ... my secret! I've always maintained that I'm not a flirt. I don't play games. If I want someone, I want someone — and I make no bones about it. No fluttering eyelashes in my arsenal.

That's what this poem's about. I wanted this guy, and he pushed all my buttons. It was yet another affair that was not to be. But oooh, I so love that feeling! You could say I'm in love with being in love.

I can still conjure up the restaurant we used to eat at in stolen moments — the food untouched, sipping a glass of wine, lost in each other's eyes. Mmm-mmm! I'll have another helping, please!

Common Denominator

Green into blue, arms entwined
Legs together, under the table
Nobody knows, nobody sees
No-one cares but us
Who would believe it?

The heat, the friction, the chemistry
Touching bodies
Reaching hearts
Finished thoughts
Minds meeting
Another world away from here

Why me?
Why you?
Why us?

Green into blue, me into you
So confused
Never understood the basics
The nature of the game
Sooner or later there's got to be
A common denominator

I was struggling with my situation in 1988. I spent a lot of time writing songs and poems, trying to relieve myself of the emotional frustration of a relationship that just wasn't working any more.

This also became a song, again unreleased, but there is a demo of it. And before anyone asks, I'm working on an anthology for release in 2014 when I celebrate 50 years in the business. All these gems will be included, I promise.

• *The picture shows the great record producer, my friend Mickie Most, and me in 1993. We had dinner at his house, and the purpose was to introduce my soon-to-be new husband. Interesting evening!*

Commitments

Attached good and tight
Stuck like glue
Both arms wrapped around
The grandfather clock

A rag doll
A kitchen table
Safe … secure
So bloody unsure

Commitments we make
Commitments we break
For better for worse
Forever

Detached, cut loose
Her mind flying
Body is free
Both arms reaching out
For lost dreams
Sex, danger
Alive, excited
So bloody sure

Commitments we make
Commitments we break
For better for worse
Forever

Here's the song from the poem. When I feel ready to write a song, I go to my poetry book. I read, I feel, I plug into Dr Creation. Usually I sit at the piano, looking at the verse in front of me, then my fingers find the keys.

I remember this one. I found the chorus first, and the rest followed quite easily. I ended the song on a hopeful note, as is my way.

I don't think there's a better way to turn a negative into a positive than to write a poem or song about it. A poem or a song isn't real to me until I type it out.

Commitments

[Quatro]

Chorus
Commitments we make, commitments we break
For better, for worse, for ever
You give and you take, so much at stake
And you're never out of danger

They say that love is anything that you want it to be
We've got to reach out, pull together, hold on to our dreams
You know that sometimes anger rises like clouds in the night
We've got to hold tight, grab the moment, let love in our lives
No more stormy skies

Chorus

They say that passion fades away, if you don't let it shine
You've got to kiss me tenderly, make it special tonight
It's true that sometimes romance dies if you hide it away
But if two people grow together, the good times will stay

Bridge
You and I, we pray for tomorrow,
Hoping, hoping to survive
All the changes of love and life

They say that love is everything if you keep it alive
And don't let strangers steal your heart
Just like thieves in the night
We've got to reach out, grow together, hold on to our dreams
You know I want you to stand beside me, you're all that I need
Cuz you believe in me

Chorus

A surprise trip, unexpected, a kind gesture ... but a little too late. The time to rekindle the romance had come and gone. I had nothing on my shelf left to sell.

It had gotten to the stage in this relationship where I had to be cruel, which is so unlike me.

Sometimes, we have no choice. One of us had to die.

And the good Catholic girl says Amen – or is it A man? Whatever! Goodnight.

• *Pictured on tour in Australia in 1985 with Laura and Richard. Nice hair cut! What was I thinking? God, where do the years go?*

Gay Paris

He lays sleeping
Not looking very healthy
Yet strangely childlike

Defences are down in slumber
I look
And begin to cry

I've put you through Hell
Guilt, recriminations
Good old Catholic know-how

But slowly, I'm beginning to believe
This was all completely necessary
Sometimes you have to kill
To survive

The bell was ringing. It was the final round. We were sleeping in separate rooms, only talking to argue, and The End was just about to be written on that page of our lives.

The line in this poem that stands out for me is Nobody wins. It's so true. There are only degrees of losing — which, by the way, ended up as the title of a song. And although it wasn't taken directly from the poem, it was taken from the sentiment.

Do I?

Angry words, nobody wins
Closed doors, night begins
Communicate, you turn away
Exterminate! Love's game in play

Who is the victor, who is the fool?
Choose your weapons in this fatal duel
Twenty paces, shoot to kill
Stormy face, break my will

Flattery, my fist too slow
Reality, cool winds do blow

Who is the victor, who is the fool
If you really want me
And I don't need you?

Angry words
Nobody wins
Closed door
Night begins

Wow! What was I doing when I wrote this — and is it legal? This would have been during the Eighties. I was playing with songs and poems all the time — exploring my religion, my feelings, my place in the world, my motherhood, basically every belief was up for grabs.

This, to me, reads like A Good Catholic Girl, way down the road.

• *Pictured at my 60th birthday celebration in Detroit are (back row) Kenny and my sister Nancy and (front row) Marilyn, me, Laurie, Terrie and Carol.*

Divine Retribution

All of our lives
From beginning to end
We pay for our sins
Then pay again

All of our nights
We pray for new dawn
In gardens of Eden
Forbid us, for Heaven's sake
Be gone

Yes, we all stand together
But we'll all fall alone
It's divine retribution
For seeds that are sown

Sins to be humble
Saints for the weak
Kings wearing halos
On Earth, for the meek

This changed shape a lot when it got turned into a song. I remember showing my poetry to my songwriting partner at the time, Miss Wolfe.

She loved "Divine Retribution" and asked me to define and explain it, so I found someone who I could use as a model to illustrate it, and it became about this man.

Without even trying, it just kind of rolled out that way. Again, he must remain anonymous, but suffice it to say, he was very important in my life.

He could be cruel, he could be kind, and I adored him ... but I could have done without so many tears.

The upside is, it toughened me up (at least, I think it did). Now, where did I put my box of Kleenex?

Divine Retribution

[Quatro / Wolfe]

You stole away all of my dignity
Everything, it was only all of me
Was I sane inside — insanity, or vanity?

Spirit breaks, walking down streets of pride
Did you mean to tell me lies? You made me cry
I cried, I cried, I cried, then I died

Chorus
What is divine, were you so kind?
Sweet revenge comes in time
Retribution is mine
(Was it divine?) I needed you
(Were you so kind?) I needed to believe in you
(Sweet revenge comes in time) I wanted to spend all the time
(Retribution is mine) Loving you
(Was it divine?) Did you mean to be so hard?
(Were you unkind?) Fill me up then tear me all apart
(Sweet revenge comes in time) Oh no-one will ever know
How I cried, I cried, I cried

Gone away, all of my quiet tears
There's nothing left but broken fears of wasted years
Wasted years, lonely tears, then no more tears

Chorus

I'm making no comment on the poem, but the picture is of a 1979 party in my honour in Detroit with the original Pleasure Seekers (my first band) – Nan, Diane, Patti and me – minus Marylou.

Instigate ... Terminate

With thine eyes of the enemy
He who conquers all
I lay down my arms
Turn my face to the wall

Clothed in coward's skin
I beg mercy ... please!
Macho Man never knows
What's hidden up my sleeve

The strength of twenty horses
I instigate
Then ...
I terminate!

Written in 1974 at Rak Records' offices. I think I was sitting in Mickie Most's room at the time.

After a year of hits, I was starting to get a little weary. I'm honest to a fault, don't know the art of bullshit, so what you see is what you get.

This particular interviewer was not nice. Baiting me on the hook of kindness and compliments. Not a very safe combination.

Interview

Interview, who's beneath this tough façade?
Me and you, who's the one who's talking hard?
Interview, me and you, interview

Here we are sitting on a Monday afternoon
Drinking our coffee in a gold and silver room
Light conversation 'bout the weather or the news
But underneath it all you hope I'll lose

You tape-record my feelings, write a bad review
Then take a picture of the pain I'm going through
My life depends upon the way you write the lines
No matter what I say, I must be lying

I'm reading down this page and wondering who I am
The way you say it like I just don't give a damn
There's no diplomacy cos no-one wants the truth
They quote you outta context, so you look the fool

Interview, who's beneath this tough façade?
Me and you, who's the one who's talking hard?
Interview, me and you, interview

Can't remember who this was about ... or even when I wrote it.

• *My good friend Berwick Kaler, best man at my second wedding, is seen here at a birthday barbecue at my house in 1994.*

Shall We Dance?

Life is full of many moments
Most of them, interrupted

So, was there a song you used to know
A melody you used to sing?

Were you young, were you hopeful
Did you believe in miracles?

And now, time is pressing
On your hopes, your dreams, your
Everything

What buttons can you press to
Kick-start life again?

This iceberg of regret will allow no warmth

Will you allow anything?
Will you allow yourself?
Shall we dance?

Sometimes I wonder where these words come from. I don't talk like this. Must have been a poet in a previous life.

I wanted to write about love, using the seasons as the different phases most relationships go through. Very pretty words, and very true.

I love putting my mind into a trance and just letting the pen flow over the paper of its own accord. Dr Creativity (mentioned before) was treating my love sickness. I hope I never recover.

Seasons

Don't forsake me, my beloved
These grey skies ordain snow
Sit … next to me
As North winds blow upon
Winter's wonder

Shake me, my beloved
From sudden rain
For the Gods have no mercy
As black storms sneak up on
Spring's thunder

Take me, my beloved
Down Lovers' Lane
Through gateways of ecstasy
Where green leaves lie soft upon
Summer's slumber

Awake me, my beloved
Though sleep I feign
Faint hearts beat expectantly
As warm breezes call upon
Autumn thereunder

Journey slowly, my beloved
Yes, all seasons come again
But treason can't pretend to be
Dreams travelling beyond
This year's blunder

All seasons come again
Yet all seasons must end
So say goodbye, my beloved, dear friend
So I may love again
We shall scatter our seeds asunder

I went through a real spiritual phase in the year I was single. Contemplated my navel, actually. Did a lot of crying, a lot of soul-searching ... sitting in my room, candles lit, music in the background, thinking and thinking and thinking.

And in the end, this poem is what I found. I found me again. Only then did I come out of my room/womb.

• *Pictured here at my granddaughter Amy's baptism, I cried like a baby.*

Solitude

A place where you live
Inside your soul
Nobody knows
Nothing shows at all
The answers you seek
Are waiting there
Right or wrong
This belongs to you

The song from the poem. This time I was showing my poetry to another songwriting partner and good friend, Shirlie Roden. This is the result.

We always sit at the piano. Sometimes I'm playing, and sometimes she is. We go back and forth, playing a chord, singing a line, stopping, listening to the creation all around us in silence until another line leaps out of nowhere.

I grab a bass, a guitar, we go back and forth ... and finally put it on to my little tape recorder. I always write in my front room, either by myself or a songwriting partner. It's the only room in the house I can create in.

Solitude

[QUATRO / RODEN]

In my solitude, where no-one dares to go
The secrets of my soul reveal what's true
In the ocean of my darkest deep desire
I know I've never loved until you
And I'm so afraid, I've crossed the line
And I'm so afraid, you will never be mine

CHORUS
Hearts on fire, I would walk the wire for you
Take you high up on a dream for two
Share the lonely, be my one and only, in my solitude
Heart's desirer, I would face the fire with you
Till I die, I give my life to you
Share the lonely, be together, only in my solitude

In my solitude I choose the dream I'm in
Confessing to the shadows on the wall
Softly whispering to hide my deepest fears
And if I cry out loud will you hear my call?
And I'm so afraid, I've crossed the line
And I'm so afraid, you will never be mine

CHORUS

In my solitude, in my silent solitude
I sit and play the strings of my heartache
In my solitude, in this bitter sweet interlude
Is the prelude the song of my heartbreak?
And I'm so afraid, I've crossed the line
And I'm so afraid, you will never be mine

Written in 1971. Waiting to fly to England. The day was looming closer and closer, and I was beside myself with hopes and dreams of what was to come. Scared, for sure, but not going was not an option.

As I say in my one-woman show, "Unzipped", my road to fame was about to begin.

• *The picture is from four years earlier and shows me and sister Arlene in a New York City hotel room, planning what naughty things we could do next.*

Suitcase Lizzie

Looking for something incredibly new
Had no particular mould
Met a magical man with a perfumed hand
Waving away the road

There I was, fresh outta school
Lonely hearts answer to super-cool
I'm Suitcase Lizzie from Detroit City
Out to try my wings
I'm Suitcase Lizzie from Detroit City
I can do anything

Floating way up in the sky
On his magic carpet
Clouds so white, rushing by
Lay back, Girl, and enjoy it
You'll never get another ride like this
Smiling sweetly, he made her sleep with a kiss

Hands encased in silver gloves
Barely touching her fingers
Electrical waves all through her veins
Imagining what he might bring her
They walked together just above the ground
Tried to speak, but didn't make a sound

There I was, fresh outta school
Lonely hearts answer to super-cool
I'm Suitcase Lizzie from Detroit City
Out to try my wings
I'm Suitcase Lizzie from Detroit City
I can do anything

My single year. The recipient was not worthy of this poem – but Hell, I wrote it anyway!

Falling in love was at the top of my list of things to do. I wanted a partner again so badly. I'd been a partner for so long and wasn't sure how to cope with not being one.

The relationship turned out to be a waste of time but, as is my way, I got a poem out of it ...

Don't be Afraid

Don't be afraid to shake
Your ground, it was never lost
Deep feelings when they quake
With honesty, are worth the cost

Don't look so scared, this falling
In love … only mountains to climb
The rope I'll hold securely
And never be far behind

What I feel for you is true
No games need I, to test
Blue eyes, may they shine through
Dark shadows, lay to rest

Afraid? Don't be, little one
Goodbyes may never be
Fear, I beg you, be released
So our spirits can fly free

I always wanted it all: a successful career, a happy marriage, and children. And I did get it all, to all intents and purposes.

But there's always a price to pay, because nobody gets a perfect life. I think the word I'm searching for is compromise ... which I did, which only I did — and that was the tragedy, because in the end you simply stop.

• The picture is of my 60th birthday celebration at Lafayette Coney Island in Detroit. I ate like a pig. The best!

Many Years Down the Road

Waiting for the storm to break
Compromise, scrutinise … then wait
Gets you nowhere, nothing but discontent

You think you've done it all
You know what you need … what you want
Too clever, I won't get trapped

Not me, cried the fool
Yet here you are, in your room, the woman's womb
Curled up in a mental foetal position

Waiting for the storm to break
The labour is long
I hope it's worth the wait

Many dreams have been sold
Many tales have been told
Many years down the road

It's important to include a poem with the same title as the book ... just like a record album. So here's mine, written in 2013.

When I was young I dreamed my dreams, and they all came true. Simply because I refused to see the world in any other way than through my eyes.

It's called believing in yourself and your vision. And that dreams can come true.

Through My Eyes

Blue patches of youth
On a denim-clad bicycle ride
Just me and my shadow
Share secrets deep inside

Soft scarlet dreams I lay upon
These pillows, oh so white
When you wish upon a star
Imagination can and will, take flight

I astral plane towards Heaven's door
Soaring higher in my mind
On the wings of an angel, I fly into
The light, leaving the rest behind

I see the world in all its glory
The story has now been told
And through my eyes I greet this life
And allow my truth to unfold

In New York, 2013, at my favourite hotel, a traditional old-fashioned place. Cary Grant lived here for years ... just fabulous.

Three o'clock in the morning. Couldn't sleep. Came out into the sitting room in front of the fireplace and wrote this.

The Warwick

Some day I will be gone, just another person
Who sat on this faded two-seater sofa
In this very old hotel room

I see the indentation on the pillows, the soiled carpet
All those lives, all those stories
Now ashes in the fabric

A dapper man, champagne flute in hand, arm resting
Oh so casual on the fireplace, surveying the room
Was he somebody's lover, or looking to be?

Silver-belled pretty lady in the corner
Jewelled neck, make-up and high heels, searching
For a pair of eyes to hold within her own

Twinkling laughter, a little too bright
Gay, frivolous, free
Desperate to keep the party flying, whatever the cost

A man crosses the room to the corner
Where the searching, beaded lady sits, waiting
Their eyes meet and touch

A chink of glasses, they sit on the faded sofa
Leaving their ashes amongst the others
In this very old hotel room

Written between 1987 and 1988. I was changing more often and more quickly than the British weather.

Simply not happy and trying to articulate to myself why I wasn't happy ... the $64,000 question.

The key line for me in the poem is "All you needed to know was the way back home."

So true.

Self-Discovery

More!
That's what your soul keeps screaming
There's got to be
More …

Once that scream is heard
The turmoil begins

Nothing satisfies any more
Five-minute conversations
You wish were twenty

He's jovial …
You want serious
Frenzied love …
You need slow

At the crossroads of life
Which way to go?

It's been one turn after another
And all you needed to know
Was the way back home

While I was assembling this book, reading the poems, doing the notes, and reliving the reasons and emotions behind the words, I realised there was one missing, one I had not written yet.

So I dredged up the most horrible year of my life when I got divorced, my mother died, and I was sad, lost, confused, scared and alone.

At some point I decided it was time to walk through the fire and take my chances again.

I'm so glad I did. This is for my husband Rainer, whom I love a little more each day. Meeting and falling in love with him is my poetic justice!

• This 1993 picture shows Rainer and me sitting on a park bench in Schwerin, Germany, where we had our first proper kiss. Ooh, it was nice!

You are My Dream Come True

I was sailing on the ocean of my life
Rocking, rolling, then crashing
Until I was marooned
With no hope of rescue

Trapped … a loveless, desolate island was I
Would anyone ever want me?
Would anyone ever need me?
Would anyone love me again?

I questioned my very existence
As the temperature dropped below zero
Forcing me to move a little closer
To the fire, burning a hole in my heart

I walked along the sandy shore
Leaving footprints of fear behind
And every step led me closer still
To that soulmate, alive inside my mind

The winds of change rushed through me
As I breathed in a life, reborn
And the hand that reached out, knew me
This orphan in the storm

We both stood, exposed and naked
As the maelstrom swirled round and round
Silent wings lifted me into the night
And we flew, to our highest ground

Among the stars we made our vows
Forever more … you and me, me and you
You are the man I dared to dream
Yes, you are my dream come true

Lightning Source UK Ltd.
Milton Keynes UK
UKHW051914090421
381726UK00002B/82

9 781910 705391